# DRIFTWOOD

prayers
passions and
permissions

Don Kimball

# DRIFTWOOD
## prayers
## passions and
## permissions

*Illustrated by Maryanne Regal Hoburg*

DOUBLEDAY & COMPANY, INC.   GARDEN CITY, NEW YORK   1978

Library of Congress Cataloging in Publication Data

Kimball, Don, 1943–
Driftwood prayers, passions and permissions.

Poems.
I. Title.
PS3561.I416D7      811'.5'4
ISBN: 0-385-13369-3
Library of Congress Catalog Card Number 77–82766

There are many who say that the true poems of our day are the songs we hear on the radio. Father Don Kimball, a priest and a disc jockey, would agree. His poetry has come unforced and unstudied between the songs he plays.

Father Don is a poem jockey who sees

> flashes of Joy
>> in rebellious flowers blooming in the rain;
>> in delirious cats swimming in a fishpond;
>> in children making mud pies;
>> in men kissing their wives;
>> in square-dancing grannies;
>> in sunsets that don't know when to quit.

Driftwood poetry.
Sometimes, on the far horizon, it is hard to tell where the sea stops and the sky begins. Sometimes Father Don is a priest on the radio. Sometimes he is a disc jockey talking to God. It's hard to know where the one stops and the other begins. In a way, all the prayers in this book are poems, and all the poems are prayers. And most important, every poem and every prayer is also a promise, not a promise made but a promise heard, that

> life is always new,
> love is always ready,
> and man
>> is
>> the
>> place
>> where
>> God
>> happens.

# Contents

## Turning In the Badge

## Joy Song

# Reach for the Sky

# *TRAVELING*

Lord, I'm on a big trip.
　　I'm a busy man.
　　　　I've got places to go, people to see, things to do.

I haven't got time to listen,
　　just time to tell you that I've got a great plan
　　　　for this world, a plan that can't miss
　　　　　　if I could just get around to the right people.

It's all in who you know, not what you know,
　　And Lord, since you and I are pretty good friends,
　　　　I was wondering if you wouldn't mind using your
　　　　　　　　　　　　　　　　　　　influence
　　　　to rearrange the world to suit my plans.

The plan calls for my getting around to enough people
　　and telling them to stop hurting one another,
　　　　that life can have meaning if they will only listen to me.
　　　　　　I could buy the key to their happiness,
　　　　　　　　and the center of their lives.

To be honest, Lord,
　　the plan hasn't worked very well so far:
　　　　People don't seem to like my plan,
　　　　　　they'd like to get rid of me,
　　　　　　　　so I need a little help from you.

What?

What did you say?

What do you mean there's only room for *one* Messiah around
　　　　　　　　　　　　　　　　　　　　　here?

# REACH FOR THE SKY

Where do people get it?

Where does love come from?

Why does love totally preoccupy my needs,
     and so overwhelm everything else I do
     that nothing has any meaning without it?

     Who is this masked marauder in my life who
          steals into my presence in the dark
          and reveals himself in the light
          as a two-armed holdup:
               the Great Heart Robbery

          "Reach for the Sky"

Lord, sometimes I think you play games with me
     —you know—
          fool with my mind, tinker with my life
     But that's OK

Since I've come to you for help
   I'm getting better mileage
      and less pollution
And I suspect that it's *my* games you're playing
   entering my life where I am
      teaching me some of your games
      —like the Great Heart Robbery—

But where do you come from?

Where is your hideout?

I really want to know.

# A TIME TO HEAL

The family once again gathers at the dinner table,
    painfully aware of the gap.

Tired and considerate parents peer across the table
    at the smaller children.

    The chatter flies
    over finger paints, test papers, and new toys.

    But the older minds wander
    and the younger minds wonder . . .
No one says the obvious:

The teen-agers are out again,
    out searching for community in a lonely world,
    for direction in an aimless peer group,
    for acceptance in a competitive culture.

Somewhere, along the jumbled journey for independence,
    often because of a confused shouting-match
        with equally confused parents,
    but more than likely because no one knew
        what to say or even how to speak,
    the important words were never said.

Tonight, suffering the empty chairs around the family table,
    the feelings are still there,
        but this time, so are the words:
        "Come home, we miss you."

## *A PRESENCE BEFORE ME*

I remember a little old lady, once, who loved to talk.
Trouble was, I was always so busy
   that I just couldn't stick around long enough to hear
     her story.

I wonder what ever happened to that little old lady.

     Forgotten by me,
       she lost her one link to the world on the outside;
     Forgotten by me,
       she no longer touched anyone else.

I still remember her.

*  *  *

I can also remember an old man who wore braces.
   He met me out in front of church one day,
     he attired in his braces, and I
       attired in all my formal church garb.
He asked me for a ride.

     I don't think I've ever met anyone who reflected a need
       and a message from God as clearly as he did that day.

     I saw the contrast between my vestments
       and his braces.
     I took him where he wanted to go.

*  *  *

7

But there have been many, many other times
   when I didn't respond, when I missed a need
      right in front of my face.

I realize now that there have been many times when I missed
   the chance to grow,
         when I missed the chance
            to touch God
         in the people
            around me.

# BOOMERANG

Lord, I'd like to see a few changes around here.

I'd like to have the world live in an atmosphere of change
    where things I don't like would give way
    to new, better ways of doing things.

I'd like to take all the polluting industries
    and put them out of business,
    so I could breathe again.

I'd make teachers more responsive to my needs,
    so I could learn again.

I'd make politicians quit playing with my mind,
    so I could understand again.

I'd take hypocrisy out of the churches,
    and drunks out of cars,
    and exploitation out of the ghettos.

I'd make a lot of changes
   if you'd give me some of that power you never seem
      to use.

Why, then, Lord, do you turn in the face of all this chaos
   and ask *me* to change?

   Look at the mess out there!!

Why do I have to do all the changing?

I'd rather rid the world of other people's pollution
   instead of mine.

Here I want to fix up this world right,
   and YOU want ME to respond to other people's needs,
      to quit playing with *their* minds,
      to deal with my own hypocrisy, drinking,
         and exploitation.

Why do you make changing so *hard???*

# WHITE HATS—BLACK HATS

Sometimes it seems like a garbage truck visits my mind
   five times a day,
      dumping on me facts and relationships
         I just can't handle.

     There I sit in the middle of my pile of debris:

     Future Shock on a Scrap Heap.

As it all hits me,
   I throw good stuff into white boxes,
      bad stuff into black boxes.

     Everything that falls on me is judged by my standards
       of acceptance, and then delivered
                         to the right department.

Lord, in your kingdom,
   are there really white boxes and black boxes?
Are there really sheep and goats,
        good guys and bad guys,
        white hats and black hats?

     I know there are many winners and losers in life,
       winners and losers by *my* standards.

     But I'm tired of narrow judgments.

Please, Lord,
   no more black and white;
     just people to love,
                 no matter how hard they hit.

# ON A WARM SIDEWALK

I saw a cat the other day, lying there on the sidewalk.
　　He just kept wiggling there on his back
　　　　totally caught up in enjoying himself
　　　　　and totally unaware
　　　　　　　of the staring world passing by.

I had two feelings about that cat:

　　　the first was the fear of looking stupid;
　　　　　everyone knows a cool cat prances, slinks, and judges,
　　　　　　　and generally looks
　　　　　　　　like he knows what he's doing;
　　　　　　　　a cool cat *never* looks stupid.
　　　　　But this cat was not cool, not together for a world
　　　　　　　of rats and mice;
　　　　　　　　this cat was really **HUNG OUT,**
　　　　　　　　and my second feeling was jealousy.
　　Way down deep, I wanted to let it all hang out,
　　　　to roll around in life till flowers bloom from my
　　　　　　concrete knees
　　　　and wind whistles through my
　　　　　　plastic elbows.
　　I'm tired of being lonely in a world
　　　　　going the opposite direction.
I want to join that cat on the warm pavement and leave the
　　　　　　　　　　　　　　　　　　　　　　　land
　　　　where cats are "cool,"
　　　　and free myself to be **ONE** with those who don't care
　　　　　　what it looks like loving warm sidewalks.
Chances are,
　　　they won't care what it looks like loving me, either.

# GIFT OF SIGHT

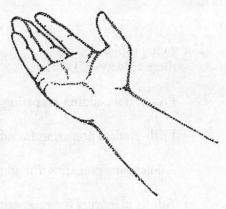

Lord, when are you going to see me, feel me,
   and touch me enough
      so that I can begin to

                    touch back in return?

      Sometimes I don't even know my own needs;
      sometimes I can't get in touch with anyone else.

I need your touch,
   tonight.

      Just as those blind men did many years ago.
        Help me, Lord, now
          to gain

           the

           Gift

           of

           Sight.

# NOW

For some people,
　　there's always a Tomorrow,

　　　　　　　　　　　　never a Today.
　　Pre-school children preparing for school,
　　　　　　　　　　next year;
　　Fifth-graders preparing for adolescence,
　　　　　　　　　　still several years away.
　　Adolescents preparing for adulthood,
　　　　　　　　　　artificially induced;
　　Adults preparing for prosperity
　　　　　　　　　　that may never come.

But who is prepared for the Now?
　　Who is prepared for now days and nights,
　　　　for now flowers,
　　　　for now sunsets,
　　　　for now people,
　　　　and now discoveries?

Lord,
　　sometimes I spend all my energies coping
　　　　　　　　　　for tomorrow's possibilities,
　　and miss today's opportunities
　　　　　　　　　that were yesterday's possibilities.

When am I going to learn that the best preparation for
　　　　　　　　　　　　tomorrow
　　　　　　　　　　is a full life today?
When will I stop praying for you to do something
　　　　　　　　　that's really mine to do?
How can I prepare for your coming tomorrow
　　　　　　　　　if I ignore your arrival today?

Let me hear your voice:

　　　　　　　　　　　　　　NOW.

# LIGHT IN THE DARKNESS

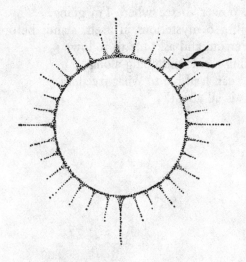

What is it about Darkness
        that takes over life
        and paralyzes me so that I can no longer move?
The Darkness from outside freezing me
                so I can't take another step forward
                        for fear of tripping, or falling
                                into a big hole somewhere.

Even more scary is
        The Darkness inside,
        paralyzing me,
        freezing me,

                        keeping me from really reaching out
                                in love,
                        from really seeing where my life
                                is going,
                        and who is out there in love.

And that's why Light can really mean something:
    Light, the power that frees me to move about,
      the power to see where I'm going.
When Light, so mysterious in itself, stands before me
    as a Person, and asks me to follow,
      taking a risk and going along
        can lead me to what freedom
        is all about.

*ZAPOID*

There's no difference between
    a person who can't see
      and
    a person who won't see.

# Troubled Man's Day

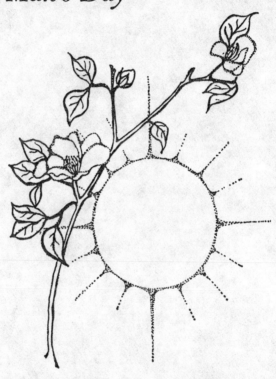

# STILL UNSATISFIED

Rivers filled with flashing fish,
Clouds filled with electric vapors,
Trees filled with teeming populations,
Rocks filled with terrestrial vibrations . . .
                              What is man filled with?

    What makes him grasp out—unsatisfied—
            for more,
            for more love,
            for more life,
            for more meaning?

Just as Unsatisfied Darkness searches for Light
                              to unlock its contents,
Unsatisfied Man seeks love,
                              life in its fullness.

He won't settle for anything else.
                              Why should he?

## BATTERED AROUND

I saw a Ping-Pong match today, Lord,
and I think I know how that ball feels:
    tossed back and forth,
    at the mercy of someone else's game.

I saw my life tossed around . . .
    disregarded by some,
    played with by others,
    given recognition only when someone else
                   wants to play games.

Lord, I don't want to be used; I want to be loved.

It occurred to me that we should use things and love people,
                  not use people and love things.

I hate games people play,
    everybody's games,
    and especially my own games,
        whether it's using people as things,
           or running in circles,
           or spacing out in escapes,
           or hiding behind masks.

Lord, will you be real enough to me
    so I can be real to myself and to others?
No games, Lord.
Just love me as I am so I can do it too.

I'm having a bad day,
And I don't want to be played with any more.

## TOUCH ME

Lord, I try so hard to show my best side,
    to act invincible,
    to cover up my mistakes.

If people saw my worst side,
    they'd run from me
    and leave me alone,
    and I can't take that right now.

I have to wear a mask to keep my friends,
    but I hurt way down deep,
    and there's no one to fix it.

Lord,
Will you help me make a few repairs below the waterline
    of my ark, where I keep my uglies carefully hidden.

    Lord, Touch my chicken legs, my vulture eyes,
        my buffalo breath, and my pack-rat heart.

        Heal my gorilla hands, my beagle ears,
        my piggy nose, and my pelican beak.

        Prime my giraffe neck,
        Pump my elbows and knees dry,
        and Quiet the hyena screech in my soul.

    And when we're done walking through the barnyard
        of my fears,
    maybe I can lift my mask a little,
    and let others into the cured part of my life.

Lord, help me.

# NERVE ENDINGS

I said to the apple tree: "Speak to me of God,"
                    and the apple tree blossomed!
I spoke to the sky and said, "Speak to me of God,"
                       and it rained.

I spoke to the road, and it accepted my wheels.
I spoke to the puppy, and he wagged his tail.

Then I spoke to the grass,
                  and it offered me a place to rest.
I spoke to the telephone pole,
        and it held up its wires of communication.

I spoke to the bird, and it soared a little higher.
I spoke to the path, and it showed me a way.
I spoke to the child, and he offered to play with me.
I spoke to the sun, and it continued to shine.
I spoke to the water, and it refreshed me.

It seemed that everything I spoke to spoke about God
  because it spoke from the center of its being.

From all ages, the world has been speaking from its core,
  while man, his ears jaded to sound,
    his eyes blurred by achievement,
      ponders God as an abstract thought,
        and then complains about His lack of presence.

Finally, on my journey, I spoke to my heart and said:
  "Speak to me of God,"
    and my heart cried out for Love.

# OFF THE HOOK

I'm sitting on a dead telephone

Only moments ago,
    The line was open
    We were in touch
    You and I shared what was real
and now, for no reason, you're gone.

It was my need to journey inward
    that brought me to open the conversation
    Dialing the code that spoke your name.

Was it something I said?

Was it something I did?

    Why did you hang up?
    It was just getting good
    And there was more to say . . .

This really bothers me.

  I'm confused.

    My soul is dark.

                Please, Lord,

                    Answer the phone.

# HOW TO DO THE GOOD-BY RIGHT

Good-bys are the hardest part of a relationship,
    a part I can never seem to get right. . . .

I announce my departure to a gathering party,
    and 45 minutes later I'm insisting—for the sixth time—
        that I'm going to leave;
And then, when a relationship gets too deep, and involvement
    appears on the horizon, my good-bys flow too easily
        from my back-pedaling psyche.
How do I do my good-bys?

Is there such a thing as being too close, and too far away?

Saying good-bys aren't that easy, I mean, using them
    to get the right distance, the right perspective
        on life, on people, on myself,
           and still not cut myself off from
               those I need, and who need me.

Why is it I say shallow good-bys to those I love,
    and empty hellos to those I don't?

Lord, am I afraid of growing . . . out to others, in to myself,
    where you really live?

Tonight, Lord, before I say good-by to another scary day,
    will you open yourself to my rainy day fear,
        my darkness, my failure,
            and show your openness to my ugly good-bys;
    then maybe tomorrow,
        I can do those good-bys a little bit better.

# CLIMB ON THE LOVE TRAIN

Lord,
Sometimes I really try to reach out,
and touch other people,
and get on the train and go where they're going,
and open myself to their world, their needs,
and what they want to do in life.

Sometimes I do help.

But what do I do with the times when I don't?
What do I do with the times when I don't even know
what I have to give?
Where do I put that feeling, Lord?
Where do I put the feeling of self-worthlessness
that creeps out of the darkness, and at times
wants to strangle me?

How do I find myself
so that the next time I climb on that Love Train
I'll be more me
and more of a giver than ever before.

I don't like being left alone in stations,
afraid of commitments,
not knowing what to give.

Teach me tonight, Lord, who I really am,
and what I really have to give.

# TENDER IN THE MORNING

Sometimes I don't think I'm going to get it right.
  I reach out in love, then I blow it,
      and I don't even know how to apologize.

Lord,
  I don't think I do my "morning-after-the-night-before"
      very well.
      My "nights-before" seem to get worse and worse;
      My "mornings-after" are getting useless.
      The point where I take up is worse
          than where I left off.

Lord, did you ever alienate anybody?
  I mean, say the wrong thing at the wrong time?
      Well, I have.
      And I guess I'd like to come to you today
          for a little advice:
      How do I reopen the negotiations
          after I've blown it the night before?
      How do I look someone right in the eye
          after I've blown it,
              and say "Good Morning! Let's start over."

Then there's your Word that
      after every death there's a resurrection;
      after every time I blow it, there will be
        a second chance;
      even if my friend doesn't forgive, you will.
        That makes it kind of nice.
      Even with other people and their limited vision,
        even with my own limited vision,
      there's a built-in safety clause here someplace.

If I just open myself a little more, try just one more time,
    you'll be there to help me through, and find my real
      Tenderness in the Morning.

## STOP AND WAIT

There are so many people today
   out on the road
   trying to find happiness "out there" someplace.

      Where am I going?
      What do I want in life?
      What do I really want to fill the emptiness
         down deep inside myself?
   If I could have anything I wanted in the whole world
      —and it didn't cost anything—
      What would I take?
      How far would I really have to go to get it?

It just seems that I am so often trying to run away *from*
                                 instead of run *into*

      relationships . . .
         . . . running away from people,
            running away from God,

running away from the very Love that could
fill
that emptiness at the bottom.

Maybe the best way is to search,
    is to stop
    and wait,
        wait for that mysterious presence to invade
        my darkness,
        to come in and search around and find
        his own place.
God somehow knows where my darkness is
        even better than I do.

# OCEAN MESSAGE

The ocean is an emperor of many moods,
    one day peaceful, mellow,
    another day wild, aggressive, accusatory.

Frankly, I'm fascinated.

    I want to come to understand this complex, oversized
        pond
            of thundering waves and gentle mist.
    I know somehow that at the core of its
        capricious fits and playful swells
            lies a treasure chest of secrets
                that can introduce me to myself
                          and
                    the meaning of life.

An ocean cannot be owned or harnessed;
    its roaring temper must never be scolded.

When relating to an ocean,
   I must learn how to wait, listen, ponder, and marvel
      at the busy regeneration going on before me
                              and
                           within me.

This is a sea that has fed me, carried me, terrified me,
   and entertained me;
      but I come back this morning for only one reason:
      my ocean has called me to freedom,
                           to relationship
                           to Life.

# A SICK CHILD

How do I love the sick child in me?
  the little insecure fearful aggressive boy
    with a garbage-can stomach
        a road-runner mind (bleep-bleep)
        a pretzel heart
    and a telescopic ego,
        who plays in my fantasy one minute
              in reality the next.

How do I love a life that's both a sandy desert of
  howling fears and an ice-blue lake of mystic satisfaction
      when people are just toys to be used,
          pounded, discovered, discarded:
      then used some more
          pounded, protected, regarded.

How do I love the little sick child in me?

Lord, one of these days I'm going to get it straight;
  I mean, I'll figure out where all the dark lonely places
      are in me,
          and let you get in with your flashlight
      to poke around and see what needs fixing.

All that darkness, all that loneliness, all that selfishness:
  a screaming tracer of empty black,
      an unlit playground of razor-blade fences
          and fluorescent manholes without covers:
              the dark side of my emotional town
                  where the sick child in me lives.

Only lately have I seen that sick child smile,
  ready again for play, for others, for life.

Lord, thank you for visiting softly, for touching firmly,
  for knowing your way around in the dark;
      you must have been there before.

Thanks, Lord.
I don't want to do my dark, sick, child alone, any more.

# WHAT DO THEY WANT FROM ME?

I know sometimes my head isn't on straight,
                    and
I know sometimes that my friends are the ones
        who know it first;
            I can tell by the way they "circle" around me, waiting
                for their chance to dart in.

It's really hard inside to look out of these creepy eyes I have
        upon people around me
            and figure them out.
                    What is my relationship with them?
                    What do they want from me?

It's even harder with a God whom I can't really see.
                    What does he want?
                    What am I doing here, anyway?
                    Why should I have to do anything in my life?
                        If he's almighty, he doesn't need me.

And Where do I put this strange message of Jesus?
        A man who came down from heaven, he said, so that I
                                            could

        be a "Co-operator" with him.
            Co-operator?
            In what?
            Something about "loving one another"
            Something about spreading around what he
                                            brought.
            I spread something around sometimes, but it's
                usually not what he brought.

I wonder if he really does need me or need anybody?
    If he does, I'd better start trying a little harder.
    I don't think I make a very good Co-operator.

Maybe
   if I could just get in touch with what he's put inside me,
Maybe that could do it.

But I'm always
   the last one to know
      when I do it
              right.

# RELATIONSHIPS

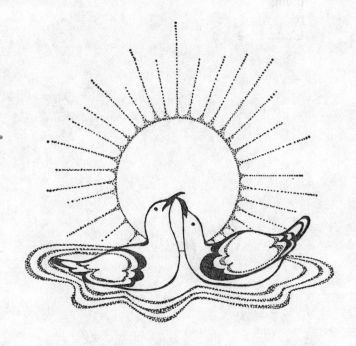

What is it about a relationship
                    that makes it
        so important in the
                    discovery of God?

Is it the fact
                that
                relationships raise feelings,
        and in discovering my feelings,
        I discover my needs,

                    and my needs point
                    to where I have to grow,

and growth
    points
    to
    God . . . ?

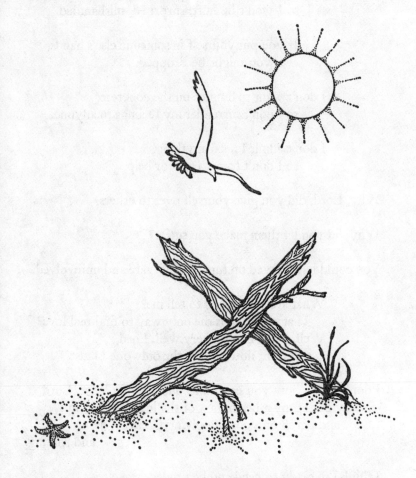

When it comes to needing others, I'm not too dependent.

I like to be on top of things:
    in football, I'm the quarterback;
    in groups, I'm the leader;
    in church, I'm the priest;
    in relationships, I'm . . .
        well, I'm not sure.

I want to be in charge, I guess, stay in control
        so I won't be hurt, surprised, mishandled.

        If you put yourself in someone else's hands,
                you might be dropped.

        I don't want to bounce on the concrete,
                so I don't surrender my feelings to anyone.

        I don't admit I need anything,
                so I don't have to ask for help.

Why, Lord, did you give yourself over to others?

Why did you let them make you suffer?

You could have stayed on top, like me: safe and uninvolved.

        What are you trying to tell me?
                That suffering is the only way to find real love?
        Well, I don't suffer very well, Lord,
                and right now, you're the only one I trust.

I don't know how you can do it, but turn me loose, Lord,
        to fly out of my asbestos nest of shallow relationships
                and perch on your life-giving Cross of giving
                                                and sharing.

I think I'm ready to need and be needed.

# TROUBLED MAN'S DAY

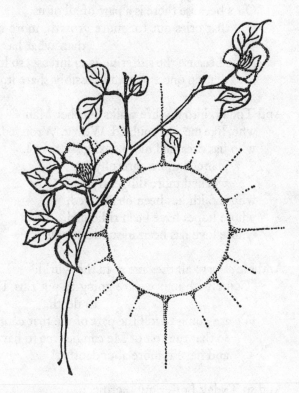

Today is the Troubled Man's Day.

Today is the day of the Weary Man, the Beleaguered Man,
   the Wronged Man, the Unfulfilled Man.

Today is the day for men
      whose dreams have not yet come true,
      whose plans have not worked,
      whose hands have not created:
         the day for men
      whose faith has been muted,
      whose hopes have been dashed,
      whose love has been rejected.

Today is our day, my day:
>    Ours because there is a part of all of us
>>    that cries out for more growth, more happiness
>>>    than what has come so far;
>    Mine because the suffering is so intense, so lonely
>>    that no one else could possibly share it.

And Today, into my life walks another Man
>    who, like me, is Troubled, Weary, Wronged, Unfulfilled;
>    who has dreamed more anxiously than I,
>>    planned more carefully,
>>    worked more diligently;
>    whose faith has been challenged,
>    whose hopes have been ridiculed,
>    whose love has been misunderstood;

And He says to all the "me's" in the world:
>    "Come with me: we are going to put this Troubled Man
>>    to death.
>    We are going to kill the part of me that cannot grow
>>    so that the rest of Me can be free to have Life,
>>    and have it more abundantly."

And so Today I offer my sacrifice:
>    and my sacrifice, my gift, is my Fear:
>    not a very pretty offering,
>    but it's a part of me;
>    And I say to my Friend: "Change it;
>    Make it more than it is now."

And Today, the day of the Troubled Man,
>    a Change, a Consecration takes place
>>    that can renew the whole world:

Today, the Troubled Man dies and my Fear turns to Peace,
>    my Peace brings Joy,
>>>    and my Joy becomes my Life.

# MY QUIETER MOMENTS

In my quieter moments
  my inner self comes forth from behind my defenses
    like dawn
    peeking from behind a tree-studded ridge.

In my quieter moments
  I sense life's rhythm,
    beating and rolling inside me, around me,
      over me, under me,
                    and
                        between me and a few special
                                          others.

In my sensitive moments
  my environment is a garden
    where I walk in the cool of early morning,
    generating magnificent thoughts,
    crafting salvific plans,
        and
    feeling at one with all that is good and real.

In my gentle moments
  I am open to anyone and everyone,
    no matter what their state of ecstasy or panic.
  I am a relational person,
    alive to others, alert to opportunity.

It's in moments like these
  I feel myself climbing, my spirit soaring off to meet
    someone
      crossing a timeless boundary,
      descending from the beyond,
      to be one with me.

It's not easy to allow myself to be quiet,
                              sensitive,
                              gentle.
Still more difficult is it to describe these moments
    to another person.
        who will usually stare back
        in sarcastic disbelief.
But I am approaching the time
    when it's OK for others to stare,
        because I am going to spend the rest of my life
                climbing
                and
            meeting my friend
                              beyond those clouds.

# EXPLODING THE CATEGORIES

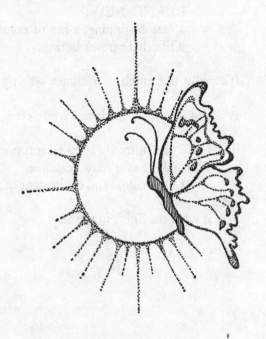

Where would we be without Spirit in our lives?

Could you imagine a relationship without Love?

Could you imagine what it would really be like
    relating to people without caring?

What about God?
What is it about Spirit that he's trying to teach us?
What is it about his power, given to us—free—
    that can make our lives different, colorful,
        exploding the black and white categories
            of our daily lives?

If we can only reach out, reach in,
    and listen to that Spirit, we are promised

A NEW LIFE,
BRAND-NEW,
a new beginning, a life of color, excitement;
a life that's never boring.

It's really not much of a choice when you think about it,
is it?
A life of stagnant, black and white categories,

. . . or
The LIFE of a butterfly released forever from the cocoon,
the tomb of everyday existence,
to the colors and excitement of flight.
That
is what the Spirit in the Sky

is all about.

# ZAPOID #2

All shit turns to fertilizer:

it's just that

the waiting

gets a little smelly.

# Turning In the Badge

## WHO IS THAT GUY?

Who is it who really calls me out to love?
    Is it just a feeling?
    Is it just the other person?
        or
    Is it just something between us,

                between us so much
                that it almost has
                its own personality,

                between us so much
                that this personality
                    seems
                    to
                    come
                    ALIVE
                  not only
              between myself
                  and
                  one other person
              but
                gradually
            between myself and many
                  other people.

# VULNERABLE

One night, I went for a walk
   past the neighbor's house,
   past the corner grocery store,
     on toward the center of town:
        playground of drunks, disease, and dirty, dingy
                      derelicts.

At first, the trouble in my own life had spun me
   into a web of concentration
        as I groped inward for an answer.

Paralyzed spiritually,
   I began to watch an old man tottering ahead of me
   stroking the sidewalk
       with strides of pride
                on legs of rubber.

My focus left him, briefly, as I considered
   the gallery of street people he passed:
        each person with his own story of pain, rejection,
                frustrated dreams.

Weird thing, though . . .
   As he deliriously tromped by,
   dark faces lit up, tense expressions relaxed;
       the street people came alive to a man of weakness
       who could touch them
             in the back alleys of their hearts.

None of the rich has produced a response like that
   in lonely men.

None of the world's power has lightened
   their load.

It took a weak, insecure, well-lathered little man
    in search of community,
            just enough fellowship to give relief from pain
                        that brought them together.

There he was: a man . . .
    morally retarded and slightly regarded
    by the "good" men of the world,
            but a breath of fresh air to underachievers
            whose stale lives had created

                                an underculture.

And I was *following* this man. . . .

That night, my search for an answer ended.

I found in this limp celebrity
    that weakness can touch more people more deeply
            than all the power-trips and human rip-offs
                        ever devised.

That night, I discovered WHY
    God's Way to touch me
        was Poverty and

                        a Cross.

## *CHANGING CYCLES*

Change is everywhere
        like
        the
        colors.

Life is shaded,
        traded,
        complicated.

The stages of our lives
        move
        like the seasons: gently at times,
                            violent here and there;
        but always determined
                        to speak
                        one
                        clear

message:
>Life leads to Death
>Death leads to New Life.

To enter the cycle,
>one must know
>>when to go up the mountain
>>and
>when to come down.

# CRYING BABIES

Crying babies drive me crazy!

The moment comes when I least expect it,
   when my coping levels are at their lowest.

   Usually I'm trapped in a plane, laced to my seat,
               or
   totally involved in a meal at a restaurant,
      delightfully unaware of the hurricane about to
         twist my innerspring
         beyond its endurance.

Then it happens:

                          a 20-lb. baby
                    with a 500-lb. scream.

My concentration vanishes,
My peace of mind shatters;
     and
My conviction that babies are cute and feelings are thrilling
   darts out the back door of my psyche,
   leaving behind a swirling fog of unfinished business
     and the nagging awareness
       that what bothers me the most about crying babies
     is that
        I
       no longer
         cry.

# STUCK IN THE MIDDLE

What do I do
    when a relationship seems to go up and down,
                    back and forth?

What do I do
    when the other person's feelings aren't the same from
                day to day?
        How do I make contact?

It seems to get more complicated when my feelings
                    aren't the same from
                day to day.

One day I close my eyes,
     and the other person is there,
          but there's a lot of hurt,

                    a lot of pain.


How do I do my confrontations in life?
     With my eyes open?


             or


                  With them shut?


And what do I do
     when I'm really not sure
       if I love that person

                   any more?

# CARING

When I care about my friends,
  I try to give them time and room to grow.

When I care about myself,
  I become possessive, dogmatic, abusive,
    and self-righteous.

Caring means reaching out in openness,
  not holding back because of fear,
  not blaming my friend for my problems,
  not rationalizing excuses as to why I'm not growing.

When I really love someone,
    I'm aware of his empty places,
        her fears, his needs.

I don't mock these places.

I try to fill them,
    and rejoice
        in the moments
            of coming together.

## POUR IT OUT

At the end of my earthly life,

      any material possessions
      or talents
      or emotional energy
            which I haven't been willing
                        to spend
                     in sharing

      will accuse me
      far more devastatingly
      than the Finger of God.

# SACRIFICE

Lord, I'd like to face it right now:

> I'm afraid of sacrifice.

> I'm afraid of anything that hurts.

When people reach out to me
   and ask me for some kind of help,

> I'm afraid!

> I'm afraid that I won't have it to give . . .

. . . which means I'm afraid
   that you haven't given me anything to give.

> How could I be so stupid!

How could I be so down on myself,
   so unwilling to recognize gifts inside of me,
      so afraid to use them!

Lord, were you ever afraid of pain?
Did you ever get so afraid of pain that you just broke out
        in a sweat?

        It seems to me I remember a place in the Gospel
                        where you broke out in a sweat.

Well then, maybe you would understand:
        I'm afraid to commit myself to anything right now, and
        I really need you to give me something special
                to recognize the gifts that are already here
                in my life,
                        so I can reach out and give them away to others.

Lord, like you who was once afraid,
        I'm scared to death of what sacrifice means
                                        in relationships.

# SOMETHING TO SAY

Have you ever been caught in a conversation
   with nothing to say?
      Staring at the other person?
      Trying to say just about anything?

            Any words that could come out would be better
               than the silence in your own heart.

Have you ever tried to listen to someone
   who had nothing to say?
      Kind of boring.

I've been thinking about my prayer life lately.
   It just seems that when God comes into my life,
      I don't know what to say.
         I don't know how to invite him.
         I don't know how to recognize him.
            And if I did, I wouldn't have any words
               to give him.

So often, my own prayer life is usually a manipulation
   of God:
         "Dear Lord, would you mind rearranging the universe
         to suit my plan?
         Would you mind using some of your almighty power
         to go along with my almighty brain?"

He's got to laugh at that!

Sometimes in prayer, I just have nothing to say.
            I wonder if sometimes he might not just take that.
            I wonder if maybe silence is the only thing
               I can offer God.

Actually, in the long run,
   *he's* the only one who really has anything to say.

# TURNING IN THE BADGE

Tonight I'm boxed in:
   the two-way door in my giving life has slammed
                                     in my face.

There is no way I can be everything to everyone.
   I'm stretched out too many ways.
      I'm tired and I'm making mistakes.

Lord, I'm turning in my Messiah Badge tonight,
   and all my ambitions with it.
      I don't want to be in charge of this world.
      I haven't got the energy to hold it together.
         A guy has to be stupid to want to be God;
         I've got too many limitations to be a good
                                 candidate.

I try to love people, and then they tell me
   I'm not doing it right. I do the best I can,
      but it doesn't satisfy them.
                          They need you, not me.

I try to understand others, but their needs boggle my mind,

entangle my heart, and then we trip and fall in a heap
   on the floor.

                          They need you, not me.

I try to read Scripture,
   but everyone has a different interpretation.
     Does being right make everyone else wrong?

I try to understand my own feelings,
   my own direction in life—you know—
   do it the way everyone says it should be done,

                              only,

I'm a very scared little retired Messiah tonight, Lord.
   I need something that I can't give myself.

               I need you, Lord, I need you.

## WHEN YOU'RE READY

God is not
    "You should . . ."

        or

            "We must . . ."

                or

                    "They'd better . . ."

                        or

                            "I ought . . ."

                            but

"I AM"

    here;

        now

           or

                later:

                    when you're ready.

# SECURITY

Inside of each of us
   lives the nagging fear
      that if we don't take care of ourselves,

                              no one will.

This fear makes us grab selfishly
   for all the things we can get in this life.
      It tells us that for security reasons

                           we must give nothing away.

As a result, our lives are spent
   scurrying around, building and protecting a world
      a shallow security,
         when, all along, a world of security and caring
            was already built, already protected

                              by God, Our Father.

To refuse his world is to deny him his creative genius.
To refuse his security is to deny him his Fathership.
To refuse his caring is to deny him any relationship to us,
   reducing him to a lonely God

                        far away and uninvolved.

Maybe today,
   we need to quit the security chase
      and to choose again the God who loves us,
         the God whose only business card

                           is the lilies of the field.

# THE MIND OF JESUS DIES

The light goes out of a child's eyes
   snuffed out by poverty, disease, ignorance, indifference,
    and just plain lack of love:
                       the Face of Jesus dies.

An unsafe coal mine explodes, trapping 30 miners inside
   in a morbid death ceremony, leaving 30 families
    with no one to care for them:
                     and the Arms of Jesus die.

An old woman, crippled with arthritis,
   no longer able to come to be used as a baby-sitter
    for the grandchildren, no longer able to walk anywhere,
     sits in a rest home—alone—in a wheel chair,
      forgotten by the family that "needed" her
       a year ago:
                   and the Legs of Jesus die.

An alcoholic lies wasted on Second Street,
   his liver gone, his hopes crushed, his stomach empty,
    longing for everything, filled with nothing:
                and the Belly of Jesus dies.

The student faced with an uncertain future,
    uncertain relationships, an uncertain culture
        that scorns belief,
                pelted in class with the dehumanization
                and eventually certain destruction of mankind,
                        wanders into a drugged escape:
                                            and the Mind of Jesus dies.


People pass one another on the street with a vacant stare:
Christians refuse an extended hand in their own churches:
Whole generations throwing emotional rocks at one another,
    each calling the other "useless":
The beat no longer goes on,
        the Heart of Jesus has stopped:
                            the Body of Jesus dies . . .
        . . . and Resurrection is our only hope.


Someone once said, "The Spirit gives life,"
And the Spirit of Jesus, untouched by death, roams the world
    . . . the way a smile roams a face,
        the way the sun tans the working arm,
        the way blood circulates in the walking leg,
        the way food nourishes the hungry stomach,
        the way Truth refreshes the mind,
        the way Love stimulates the beat of the heart,


But the Spirit needs a Body to live in, a Body to give life to;
And we have a Body that needs life, needs it more abundantly.

I wonder if we can get them together soon,
                        and produce an Easter Resurrection.

*PONDEROID*


## IF GOD ESTABLISHED HIMSELF IN MAN

## WHY CAN'T MAN ESTABLISH HIMSELF WITH
## MAN?

*Joy Song*

# LONELY-LOOKING SKY

In a world with people staggering about
      in a lonely search for happiness,
there is no more lonely place than pre-dawn darkness
      looking for the first light from the rising sun.

Across the lonely-looking sky,
        the night's emptiness stretches forth its arms
          to drink the pink-liquid light,
        reassuring itself that the dark terror
          of nocturnal fears will fade before daylight's
            awesome power.

Who is it
    who could set before us such a clear message
      about our lives?
Only the One
        who created the consoling mystery of light
          over darkness,
        of gentleness over harshness, and
        of vision over blindness from within.

The sky is lonely only for the sun
        to come to complete its existence
  and
        give it meaning.

## JOY SONG

There's got to be more to life
   than what we've experienced so far:
                    50 billion maggots can't be all wrong!

What if they gave a hell, and nobody came?

What happened to the "hundred fold" in this life?

Don't tell me the Greatest Story Ever Told
                    has a crummy ending!

There has to be Joy somewhere in the middle of all this mess!
   a Joy that's not oblivious to pain;
   a Joy that recognizes grief, but moves beyond it;
   a Joy that says it's OK to cut loose and be me,
                    and like it!

I've seen flashes of Joy
   in rebellious flowers blooming in the rain;

in delirious cats swimming in a fishpond;
in children making mud pies;
in men kissing their wives;
in square-dancing grannies;
in sunsets that don't know when to quit;

Flashes that say:
    Somewhere,
    Someone's really enjoying this life
        and having more fun than just a joke
        and more peace than just laughter
        more moment than just the passing
                    of a good time.

Joy is myself in touch with the best of everything . . .
    . . . even when it only happens once in a while.

# DISCOVERY

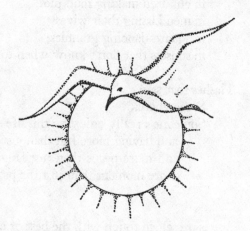

Summer is the settling of the Winter of Discontent,
and digging my way from my cave of spiritual
hibernation,
I find that the summer sun has shed light
on a few questions I used to wonder about.

It just came to me one day that
To Believe is to reach out in the darkness
and ask for a cure;

To Hope is to be in the constant state of discovery;

To Love is to be responsible for someone,
to sacrifice oneself for someone,
to risk and to share;

To Pray is to receive God's Communications,
to be attentive,
to listen;

To Be in Grace is to let things and people happen to us
while God slips in among them;

To Worship is to celebrate all of this as best we can,

   for "Nothing is profane
               for those
                        who know how to see."

# FEELINGS

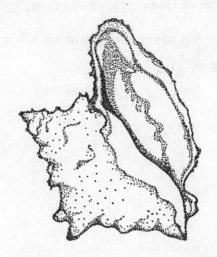

Lord, I learned a long time ago not to trust my feelings.
Feelings were bad; they were always suspect.
After all, everyone knew that nothing came of feelings,
                                    except evil.

    When I yelled as a kid, just because I felt like yelling,
        I was squelched: "Mommy has a headache."
    When I cried, I wasn't being very grown-up:
        I wasn't being a man.
    When I laughed, I upset those older people
        who had long ago forgotten how to laugh,
                forgotten how to feel.

    Soon I became like them: no more yelling,
        no more crying, no more laughing.
    The silence outside lied about
        the yelling, crying, laughing chaos inside.
    I had become a polite, well-groomed lie,
        living up to everyone else's hang-ups,
        but never faithful in dealing with my own.

Then some people came into my life:
   maybe you sent them to me, or maybe they were there
      all the time,
         I finally just heard them.
Anyway, they were real people,
   alive to what they saw, what they felt.
      They showed me life from the feeling side.
And now, Lord, for the first time
   like the first man,
      I see CREATION—I see flowers,
                     I see mountains and streams
and best of all, Lord, I see people not just with my eyes,
   but with my feelings.
      I see PAIN—oh, do I see pain,
         but Lord, I see Love there too.


And now, for the first time, I think I can see and hear you.

# *LOOKING BACK*

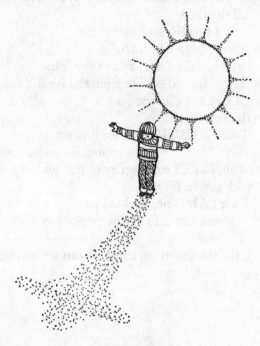

I can remember one time when I was very young,
   I guess I was about four, I was playing
      with a little friend of mine out by a swimming pool
         half full of water.
Like all kids, we went exploring into the pool.
   The shallow end didn't have any water in it,
   And we were playing soldiers.
       Then I came too close to the drop-off
         and I slipped into the muddy water at the deep
                          end.

I can still remember that day.
I can still remember my friend running off to get help,
   with help arriving just in time
      in the person of a teen-age neighbor who jumped in
         and pulled me out.

Looking back now, I can see God making up for damage
   I almost did to myself,
      out of the carelessness of my youth.

* * *

I can remember my first burial: my own cousin, killed
   in Vietnam.
      That was the saddest day of my life.

I really reached out for something special to give
   my own family.
      After all, as a priest, I had something to give them,
         but that day I had trouble finding it,
            because of my own grief.
   But I gave it because God put it there to give.
      It didn't come from me.

* * *

I can remember many happy times,
   one being the day I met my first disc jockey.
      It was at a bongo concert in Santa Rosa;
         One of the big San Francisco disc jockeys was up.
Would you believe I won third place,
   and had never beat on a bongo drum in my life?

* * *

Were you there, Lord,
   when I was touched by "a little extra" in my life?

# SUMMER

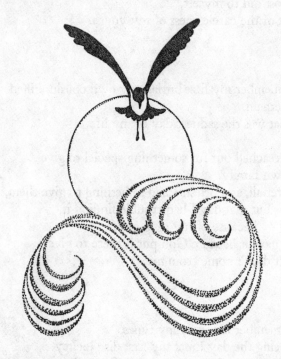

It's summer, Lord,

      and that lazy feeling is coming back.

Summer is the time for aimless walks
           through rambling fields,

           taking time to watch
              jackrabbits and bees,

           whole acres of curiosity.

I'm curious about their careless existence:

all they seem to need is food.
      And they're wondering what *I'm* doing
                             there.

You said something about the lilies of the field once,
      how they don't work and are still cared for,
                        yeah,
      and about sparrows, and how I'm worth
        more than hundreds of them.

      Did you really mean that?

You mean, I don't have to earn your love,
      just take it?
                        Free?

      That's all right!

It's summer, Lord,
And I don't feel like working anyway.

I could use a little of that unearned love.

Maybe that's what I've been missing in my life.

# THE CURTAIN GOES UP

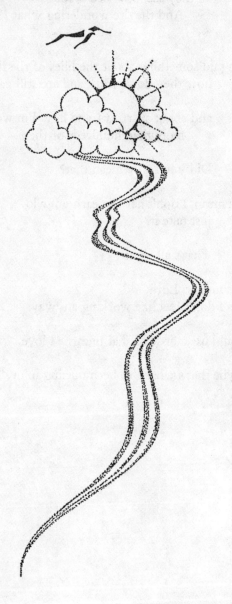

Light's early morning fingers
   chase shadows across the treetops as
         sunshine once again takes possession of the day.
Gracefully, the grey night surrenders her starry cloak
   to the Pillar of Fire journeying from the East.

Joyous birds streak across pastel skies,
   chirping the musical accompaniment to the full, sensual
         drama that all creation is once again presenting.

Forest animals move shyly to their places
   as rocks glisten and giant redwoods tremble.

It is the people who perhaps have missed a cue,
   playing observers when we are fully ourselves only as
         participants speaking the crucial love-lines
               which bring to this magnificent background
               a central theme.

The theme is caring for ourselves, for others, for all of life.
   The plot handed to us is a mystery of love received and
         then shared, recycled, passed on to others.

We speak only what we hear spoken to us.
We give only what is given to us.
We search out in others only what was called forth from us.

As the day breaks once again,
   warmth creeps back into our psyches, reminding us
         that we can still be as fully alive and fully loved
               as we allow ourselves to be.

# PUSHING AWAY

Sleep is the door to my basement of spiritual terrors,
   a Door I can close as the summary of my day's encounters
      swirls toward me like a herd of munching tornadoes
         ripping up my feeling structure
         and flinging it into some God-forsaken, foggy
            swamp.

As my Door closes on my ever-increasing realization
   of my role in people's lives,
      I find myself—at last—pushing away from the day,
         back into my interior world
         where the skies are always blue,
         where the beaches are always warm,
         and where the good guys all wear white hats.

   This is my "other side"
      where fantasy becomes reality
            and reality becomes symbolic:
                    DREAMLAND,
      fully equipped with the latest in Fairy G.M.'s.

I'm only now hearing my need to be alone
   as a thing truly acceptable in my life.
Compulsive fantasy is an illness to be feared,
   but not the world of *chosen* fantasy
      where trips to the inner world, naturally induced,
         can bring me to an encounter with myself
         and with God that cannot be explained adequately
                  to anyone.
         For someone who hasn't been there,
           there are no words of explanation.
         For someone who has been there,
           there is no need for such words.

Pushing away is now becoming part of my daily routine,
  a pause in the day to collect myself,
      to ponder the wisdom of the Scriptures,
     and to drink the energy that seeps out of patient
                         redwoods
          or glides toward me from people
          who seems to know and understand
              that my destiny is still between me and God,
              a course continuously being charted
              in our encounters within my whited
                      sepulchre:

          still black in places, still holding
              some dead man's bones,
        but still—as always—a place to push away
            from death
          and greet the world with my resurrected
          **NEW LIFE.**

# THE GUITAR MAN

Listen to the music,
> and you will hear something stir in your soul.

It stirs simplicity in the midst of complexity;
it streaks like sunlight on a cloudy sky:
> like a voice that doesn't have to talk to be heard:
> like a hand that doesn't have to touch to be felt.

There's something strangely familiar in that melody
> like hearing a person you've seen for the first time,
> and yet you know you've met him somewhere before:
> THE GUITAR MAN.

His Guitar freaks its way across time-honored arrangements,
> lifting men from beds of apathy,
> resurrecting them from premature death,

> constructing a strange harmony
> > between the old and the new; between left and right;
> > > black and white;
> > joining empty to full; and crawling to running;
> > bringing self-awareness to the selfish,
> > > relationship to the lonely, life to the dead.

There's something strange—about the Guitar Man
> in this orchestra . . .

something strange—like the voice of God.

Listen to the Music:
> He will speak again.

# WHERE DOES HE LIVE?

Think of all the money
    that has gone into
        the buildings of Christian Worship
Buildings that have been the source of inspiration
    down through the centuries.

    And then think of the temple to
        human misery and poverty
    which has outlasted the strongest buildings. . . .

        And then you will know why God
            took up His dwelling
        in the human temple.

In Jesus Christ,
    God is a poor man;
        He is the economic problem we have never solved;
He is
    my brother.

## CLOSE TO THE WATER

Water has always been
  a symbol of fascination to man.
      Somehow, in approaching water,
        he comes at rest with the center of his being,
        he learns to relax,
            and not have to get up and go. . . .

It's here that a person not only finds his own center,
  but at the root of that, even,
      he finds the presence of God.

      Maybe that's why Jesus was so close to the water,
        walking around it and upon it,
        calling us out of our boat of safety
        to walk on it with him . . .
          walking to the center of our Being
           to be there with him . . .
              . . . and share his peace. . . .

If we're going to learn the secret of Being
  as Living,
      we're going to have to remain
              close to the water.

# LOSERS

It seems so funny how we get trapped up in rushing around,
   trying to achieve,
   trying to score in some way
        to make our own inner self feel a lot better.

When we get trapped in this rushing about,
   we start basing our whole value system on performance:
     when a person does something right,
                 he's given 10 points:
     when he blows it,
               he doesn't get any at all.
  We lay this value system on other people,
   and begin demanding that they perform in the style we
                        do:
  after a while, the misunderstandings that result
   become something that can't be tolerated any more.

Here we are: a society that's rich,
  we have resources that seem endless.

And yet, we're victims of the very same rushing around
    that *could* teach us that
        maybe we ought to slow down:

        maybe *Being*
          is a lot more important
          than *Doing*.

People who don't achieve in society,
   the "losers,"
      maybe they're not so bad off.
      When they blow it sometimes,
        maybe they're not really
                blowing it.

# HEARTBEAT

The sound of the human heartbeat
    is one of the most thrilling sounds in existence.

    It is the core of a person's rhythm
                in stride with the pulse of life.

The sound of one person's beat is in foot-tapping
                    or
                        finger-snapping;
    another person keeps time with word-cadence
                    or
                        head-bobbing;
    Some swing,
        some bounce,
            some wiggle.

The North Coast rises to another morning
        checking its pulse.

        The day will be upbeat,
            downbeat,
           or
           offbeat;
But everyone will move to the beat of an inner drum.

From all ages,
    mystics have spent their lives measuring their heartbeats,
                      their pulses,
                    their rhythm.

    The inner journey toward God
        will always lead the pilgrim
        across the plaza of his own emotional town
        in search of his spiritual identity.

The day he discovers his personal pulse
beating in harmony with another,
he may paint the world
the color of the heart,
for
he will then know
Love
by its first name.

## MASKS

Sometimes it comes in the morning;
    more often, late at night:
                    The feeling of worthlessness;
                    the nagging suspicion
                        that
                        at the center
                            of my person
                                nothing
                                is
                                there.

No one must know,
    so I wear a mask,
        my way of showing people
            a value I don't really feel.
    But my masks look like warty frogs,
            sightless in my muddy puddle of relationships
            an easy target for puddle-stomping kids.

The cure isn't in changing masks,
                substituting a new one for an old one.
It's in letting someone into my emptiness,
        receiving their kiss of acceptance
            and
        being released to see
            that being empty
                only means being ready
                    to be filled with
                    love,
                    peace,
                    and
                    God.

# SHALOM

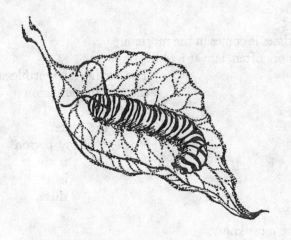

The cocoon is quiet,
  the bug
    wrapped
    in a homespun security blanket.

Copping out?

Hardly.

Only waiting
    changing,
    becoming.

Soon a blooming moment,
    a resurrection flag-waving
      as wings unfurled
      proclaim new life,
          new vision,
          new mobility.

Only a crazy caterpillar
              hearing a tone
                        no other insect hears
              dares
              defy the world of strugglers
                  and
              peacefully
              wrap
              and
              wait
              "losing" his life
              to possess his wholeness.

# CATERPILLAR

So many things in life are just a big paradox.
Take the paradox of the little caterpillar crawling
   along the ground,
     just a little somebody that always seems
       to get stepped on.
   But somehow he carries something within him that speaks
     of greater things than just an old caterpillar:
         it's the power to become
            a butterfly,
       a spirit within him that can be released
        if he is willing to die to himself.


Maybe that's what the Spirit of God is all about:
        hanging on for dear life,
          even when we look like we are in a cocoon;
        hanging on until we are released
           in color and in flight.

# HUMBOLDT COUNTY NEW YEAR

Out of icy clouds and frosty peaks,
   a river winds down the mountain,
     pouring into gorges, and spreading fingers of latticework
       through soggy green fields.
The river knows where it's going; it has its own momentum.

Overhead, a bird loiters on quiet currents of air,
   clean, fresh air,
   then cruises easily across scenic vistas.

The New Year has come to Humboldt County.
But for mountains and birds, streams and fish, nothing
   is really new.

We are the ones who need a New Year
   to leave behind old mistakes,
   to heal broken relationships,

to find new sources of energy to convey us to new places,
                                            new relationships,
                                                new beginnings.


We begin this year jealous of majestic birds
    who know their energy source and use it wisely.
We begin this year angry at others who have wasted *our*
                                        energy,
    but conscious, when we are honest with ourselves,
    that we have wasted our own material energy
    and what's worse, our psychic, spiritual energy as well.
            Waiting for the Arabs, the South Americans,
            or even the Oil Companies won't help us solve
                the real energy crisis:
                    the love crisis in our lives.
                Loneliness is an energy crisis.
                Emptiness is an energy crisis.
                Hate is an energy crisis.

                Our hearts are the only fuel pumps:
                    they never run dry,
                    they just get tired.

On this great morning after the year before,
    it is good to know that
                life is always new,
                love is always ready
                    to boost, to cheer, to forgive, and to
                                            begin again.

# MESSAGE

The next time

    I look

        for God,

            I won't

                think;

                    I'll listen.

# CHRISTMAS STAR

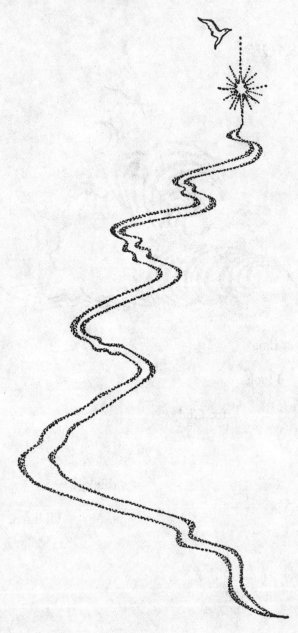

Across the world once again, a star is in our sky,
                                a gift is in our hearts:
                                                it's Christmas.


Right here in Humboldt County
        Highway 101 is our backbone,
        Our rivers our arms and legs.
        The forest is our clothing.
        The ocean is our blood.
                                As a people, we have known
                                        struggle, isolation,
                                                darkness, and bitterness.
                                But more important,
                                        we have also found success,
                                                security, happiness,
                                                        one another.


It's Christmas once again:
        time to focus on what makes light overcome darkness
                and love overcome emptiness.
It's time to believe once more that
        no matter how battered our lives are,
        no matter how well off we are materially,
There is still someone who knows our darkness and lights it,
                                who knows our hurt and heals it.


It's a moment for healing,
        and we really need it this time.
                Healing is the medicine that can close the wounds
                        between parent and child, brother and sister,
                                government and people.
                Healing comes from God
                        directly or indirectly.


We must do what we can do;
He does the rest.

# THANKS

Lord,

I just want to say "Thanks" tonight for being patient with me.

A lot of my friends get so uptight with me when I run
    in and out of relationships trying to find myself.

In my lonely search, I find I fall out of relationships
    more easily than I get in. . . .

       But that's me right now, I guess.

Some people can't accept that in me yet.
You're different, Lord, from all the people around me;
You don't force the issue.

       You have the patience of forever,
       You have carved out mountains with glaciers of ice,
       You have seen the giant redwood grow from a seed;

       You, Lord, have been my friend all along,
          offering relationship,
          but never forcing it.

       All along, you have been the one there,
          ready when I was,
          offering what I could take,
          taking what I could offer,
          and changing it back into Yourself.

Thanks for being with me until I was grown up enough
                         to be with you.

I think I know what it means—in the best sense—
to be dependent.

You're all right!

*PONDEROID #2*

MAN

IS

THE

PLACE

WHERE

GOD

HAPPENS

Many people have encouraged me to write, but I never seem to get around to it. I have a terrible habit of never answering mail: "no time." This book is a collection of reflections and prayers created under pressure: I needed material for my radio show.

I never would sit down and write a book, but I find, over the past five years, that I have written one. It is the product of many relationships with people who have offered me the chance to know them, and who have called my "real" self forth from inside. I have grown from joy as well as pain. For all the people in my life, I am deeply grateful.

As for this book I am particularly thankful for:

God, who had to hear these prayers the first time;

KATA, my radio station in Arcata, California, which has supplied me a disc-jockey chair and a lot of friends;

KFRC in San Francisco, who proved to me that people can still care, even in a high-performance business;

Tom Farrell, who believed in this book before I did;

Maryanne Hoburg, my illustrator, who reveals and shares as a way of life;

The Catholic Youth Organization staff and teen-agers of Humboldt County: my reason to grow;

My deepest and closest friends who have believed so much in me: my courage to grow.

Don Kimball